ANIMALS ON THE BRINK

Polar Bears

Don Middleton

www.av2books.com

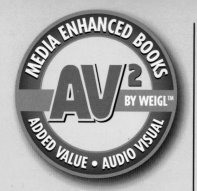

AV² provides enriched content that supplements and complements this book. Weigl's AV² books strive to create inspired learning and engage young minds in a total learning experience.

Your AV² Media Enhanced books come alive with...

 Audio
Listen to sections of the book read aloud.

 Key Words
Study vocabulary, and complete a matching word activity.

 Video
Watch informative video clips.

 Quizzes
Test your knowledge.

 Embedded Weblinks
Gain additional information for research.

 Slide Show
View images and captions, and prepare a presentation.

 Try This!
Complete activities and hands-on experiments.

... and much, much more!

Go to www.av2books.com, and enter this book's unique code.

BOOK CODE

V478201

AV² by Weigl brings you media enhanced books that support active learning.

Published by AV² by Weigl
350 5th Avenue, 59th Floor
New York, NY 10118
Website: www.av2books.com   www.weigl.com

Library of Congress Cataloguing in Publication data available upon request.
Fax 1-866-449-3445 for the attention of the Publishing Records department.

ISBN 978-1-61913-429-4 (hard cover)
ISBN 978-1-61913-430-0 (soft cover)

Printed in the United States of America in North Mankato, Minnesota
1 2 3 4 5 6 7 8 9   16 15 14 13 12

062012
WEP170512

Project Coordinator Aaron Carr
Design Mandy Christiansen

Every reasonable effort has been made to trace ownership and to obtain permission to reprint copyright material. The publishers would be pleased to have any errors or omissions brought to their attention so that they may be corrected in subsequent printings.

Photo Credits
Weigl acknowledges Getty Images as its primary photo supplier for this title.

Contents

Take a Stand
· Debate ·
· Research ·

How to take a stand on an issue **5**

Photos of polar bears often **17**
show the animals in groups,
even though group behavior is
limited. Is it wrong to portray
polar bears as social animals?

Should we stop drilling for gas **29**
and oil in the areas where
polar bears live?

Does the number of polar **33**
bears show that Earth's
environmental problems are
getting worse?

The Polar Bear

On the ice of the **Arctic**, a polar bear is an awesome sight. A polar bear is the size of a small car. Its shoulders are almost as wide as a single bed. This book will explain what these big bears eat, the way they hunt, and how they interact with other animals. You will read about polar bear cubs and find out why the polar bear's survival is in question.

The Inuit and other peoples of the North have lived with polar bears for thousands of years. The rest of us are just beginning to understand these large **mammals**. Read on to find out why polar bears deserve their Inuit name, *Nanook*, which means "ever-wandering one."

The polar bear is the largest of all bears in the world.

Polar bears descended from the ancestors of brown bears.

How to Take a Stand on an Issue

Research is important to the study of any scientific field. When scientists choose a subject to study, they must conduct research to ensure they have a thorough understanding of the topic. They ask questions about the subject and then search for answers. Sometimes, however, there is no clear answer to a question. In these cases, scientists must use the information they have to form a hypothesis, or theory. They must take a stand on one side of an issue or the other. Follow the process below for each Take a Stand section in this book to determine where you stand on these issues.

1. **What Is the Issue?**
   a. Determine a research subject, and form a general question about the subject.

2. **Form a Hypothesis**
   a. Search at the library and online for sources of information on the subject.
   b. Conduct basic research on the subject to narrow down the general question.
   c. Form a hypothesis on the subject based on research to this point.
   d. Make predictions based on the hypothesis. What are the expected results?

3. **Research the Issue**
   a. Conduct extensive research using a variety of sources, including books, scientific journals, and reliable websites.
   b. Collect data on the issue and take notes on all information gathered from research.
   c. Draw conclusions based on the information collected.

4. **Conclusion**
   a. Explain the research findings.
   b. Was the hypothesis proved or disproved?

The Bear Basics

Polar bears have a layer of fat that can be 4.5 inches (11 centimeters) thick. The fat can be used for energy if the bear cannot find food. It also helps keep the animal warm.

Polar bears shed their fur once each year, during the summer. This helps them stay cool in the warmer weather.

Features

Polar bears are covered with a dense, heavy fur. They have fur everywhere on their bodies except for their broad, black noses and the rough, black pads on the bottom of their paws. A polar bear's fur can be pure white, but it is usually more of a creamy yellow color. The color is excellent **camouflage** for the bear when it hunts its prey in areas covered with snow or ice. Scientists have discovered that each strand of the polar bear's hair is transparent. This means that light rays from the Sun can pass through the hair and reach the bear's skin. The sunlight helps keep the animal warm.

A polar bear's coat is made of two layers of fur. Close to the body, there is a dense, woolly undercoat. Above that is an outer layer of long, coarse hair, called guard hair. An oily coating on each guard hair helps keep out water. When a polar bear comes out of the water, it shakes its body as a dog does to remove all the water from its fur. Dry fur protects a polar bear better against the cold.

Polar bears are closely related to brown bears. The head and ears of a polar bear are smaller, in relation to body size, than those of a brown bear. Yet the polar bear is larger overall. The neck and body of a polar bear are longer than those of any bear. Of all land animals, polar bears are the largest **predators** on Earth. An adult male polar bear, measured from the ground to the highest point of the shoulder, is usually about 3.3 feet (1 meter) tall. Some of the largest male bears are up to 5 feet (1.5 m) tall. Measured from the tip of its nose to the end of its short tail, an adult male polar bear may be 8 to 10 feet (2.4 to 3 m) long. Male polar bears normally weigh 25 to 50 percent more than females. Adult males can weigh from 750 to more than 1,500 pounds (340 to 680 kilograms). They are heaviest in the late spring or early summer. They have grown fat eating newborn seal pups during the previous three months.

Many young polar bears do not live to be adults. They die from a number of causes, including disease, starvation, and attacks from adult male bears. Of those that do survive into adulthood, only a few polar bears live longer than 20 years in nature. The oldest known polar bear in the Arctic lived to be 32 years old. In zoos, polar bears have an easier life. If they get sick, a veterinarian can care for them. Many captive polar bears live longer than 30 years. Some have even lived to the age of 40.

Classification

Bears belong to the **family** of animals called *Ursidae*. The family is part of an **order** that includes tigers and dogs. Scientists use Latin words to name animals. *Ursus* means "bear." It is not surprising that the polar bear's Latin name, *Ursus maritimus*, means "bear of the sea." These Arctic bears spend more time in the water than any other bear. Scientists believe that polar bears developed from the ancestors of brown bears roughly 500,000 to 750,000 years ago. The first polar bears appeared during the late Pleistocene period. During the Pleistocene period, the temperatures on Earth were much colder than they are today. Thick layers of ice covered much of North America and northern Europe, as well as parts of Asia and South America.

Scientists who study **fossils** think that some ancestors of brown bears became isolated and trapped in ice-covered northern areas. Instead of dying from hunger and cold, these bears learned to hunt seals. They developed into a **species** better able to survive on the **sea ice**. The ice sheet stopped advancing southward about 18,000 years ago. As the ice began to retreat to the north, polar bears and seals moved northward with it. Today, polar bears are well adapted to their environment in the Arctic.

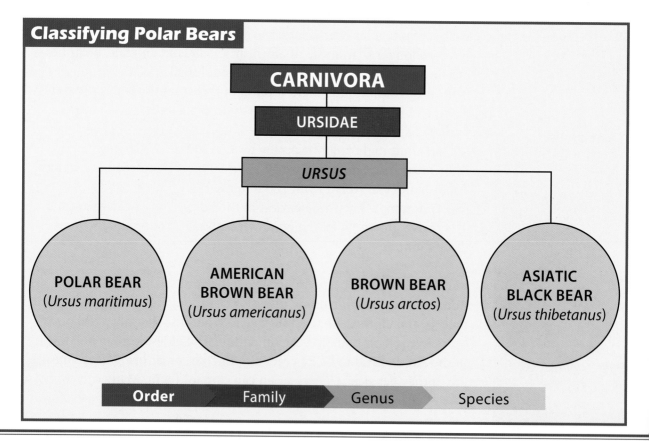

Classifying Polar Bears

```
                    CARNIVORA
                         |
                     URSIDAE
                         |
                      URSUS
```

| POLAR BEAR (*Ursus maritimus*) | AMERICAN BROWN BEAR (*Ursus americanus*) | BROWN BEAR (*Ursus arctos*) | ASIATIC BLACK BEAR (*Ursus thibetanus*) |

Order → Family → Genus → Species

When polar bears swim underwater, they are able to close their nostrils and flatten their ears to keep water out.

The American brown bear is like a cousin to the polar bear.

The polar bear's thick fat is distributed fairly evenly across its body. The fat actually helps the animal float and swim in water.

Special Adaptations

Over thousands of years, polar bears have developed many special features that help them live and hunt where it is cold. In fact, polar bears overheat very easily when the temperature is above freezing.

Eyes

A polar bear's eyes can filter the Sun's glare on snow. The bear's eyes are rounded, but they flatten when the polar bear is swimming underwater. This helps the bear see underwater with open eyes.

Nose

Polar bears have longer noses than other bears. Polar bears use their sense of smell to find seals. A polar bear seems to be able to smell a dead whale body more than 1 mile (1.6 kilometers) away. Polar bears also use their sense of smell to find potential mates from tracks in the snow.

Teeth

Polar bear teeth have sharp, jagged edges. This allows polar bears to rip off bite-sized chunks of **blubber** and meat, which they swallow whole rather than chew. The **canine** teeth of a polar bear are used for gripping and tearing the hides off its prey.

Ears

A polar bear has excellent hearing, even though its ears are small. The ears have fur on the inside as well as the outside to protect them from freezing. Their size is helpful because little body heat can be lost through small ears.

Paws

Measuring up to 12 inches (30 cm) across, a polar bear's paws work like snowshoes to help the bear stay on top of thick, crusty snow. On the bottom of the paws, rough black pads help polar bears walk and climb on slippery ice. When swimming, polar bears use their front paws as paddles. The smaller and narrower rear paws are used as **rudders**.

Claws

Each toe ends with a curved claw about 3 inches (7.5 cm) in length. The claws are thick, strong, and black. They do not **retract**. The claws are used to catch prey. Their sharp tips also help prevent polar bears from slipping when traveling across ice.

Groups

Polar bears live in the Arctic, where temperatures are below freezing most of the year. Their group behavior changes with the seasons. Adult male polar bears live alone when hunting seals on the sea ice. During the summer and fall when most of the ice has melted and some bears are stranded on land, the bears are sometimes seen together. Otherwise, polar bears are not often found in groups. Polar bear groups occur most often during the summer, when more of the bears are forced to live on land.

During the three to four months of summer, the bears wait for the ocean to freeze again. Some of the male bears will make friends during this period. They will play fight with one another and even rest and sleep together. This may continue for several weeks. Polar bears have even been seen hunting together out on the ice for a short period after the ocean starts to freeze. They then go their separate ways as the ice forms again. It is usually younger polar bears that form a temporary group.

Polar bears seldom fight with one another. They have established a natural order, or way of relating, which is quite simple to figure out. Larger bears are usually more **dominant** than smaller bears. Male bears are most often dominant over females, except when a female bear has cubs at her side. Female polar bears spend most of their lives raising cubs. A mother will often fight to the death if a male bear tries to harm her cubs.

Young bears give way to the adult bears. Sometimes a large bowhead whale, a beluga whale, or a narwhal dies, and its body washes up on shore. Many bears come to feed on the dead animal. Usually, the bears do not fight because there is plenty of food to share. If a very large bear comes along, smaller bears simply move aside and wait their turn.

The older males spend most of their time alone throughout the year.

The Bear Basics

Only female polar bears that are expecting cubs will go into a den for a long time during the winter. While in the den, the females do not eat, drink, or pass their waste.

Unless it is mating season, polar bears tend to avoid confrontations.

The Bear Basics

To signal that they want to play, polar bears will often wag their heads from side to side. Then they will stand on their hind legs and lower their chins.

Adult polar bears sometimes pretend to battle. Their mock fights are like sporting events for bears.

Communication

Unlike humans, polar bears cannot change their facial expressions very much. Instead, polar bears have developed other ways of communicating. Using sounds and body language, polar bears show other bears their mood, such as when they are angry or upset. At times, the bears seem to make friendly sounds as a means of greeting one another. When a submissive bear is interested in the food that a dominant bear has, the smaller bear will circle the prize slowly. If both bears are ready to share the meat, they will often touch noses. This is the way the bears greet one another.

Males have been seen making soft sounds around females that they are interested in mating with, and the females make sounds in response. Polar bears are most likely to make noise when they are feeling anxious or threatened. Some of the sounds made by polar bears are described as chuffs, woofs, grunts, snarls, and roars. The bears also hiss and make chomping sounds with their teeth. Mother bears make sounds of warning when their cubs are in danger. These include a kind of braying and a chuffing sound. Observers have often noted that cubs are able to pick out their mother's voice.

Polar bear cubs will whine, squeal, and whimper when they are upset. The cubs are the ones who make sounds the most often. They produce sounds to express many emotions and needs. The cubs make a humming sound called a nursing chuckle when they are content, such as when they are feeding on their mother's milk. They whimper and sometimes smack their lips. Young cubs often hiss at one another and make sounds deep in their throats.

The bears also give and get messages using their senses of smell, sight, and touch. Scientists who study polar bears are able to understand many of these signals. Researchers have noted that submissive bears seem to try to stay downwind of dominant bears. Mother bears snuggle their cubs to protect and encourage them. The mothers will also show their displeasure or even punish their offspring by swatting at them. Years ago, scientists thought that if two bears were confronting each other, they were fighting. Researchers now believe that this is often just a form of play fighting.

Body Language

All bears use body language to communicate to other bears how they are feeling. Although polar bears keep to themselves for much of the time, they have ways of signaling their feelings when they are together. Posturing, or displaying the body to other bears, is an important kind of body language. This kind of body language allows bears to safely judge one another's moods and avoid fighting.

Submission

A large polar bear will often turn its body to the side and stand tall. This allows another bear to see how big it is. A smaller bear will give way to the larger bear by lying down, keeping its head lowered, and avoiding eye contact. The submissive bear may also move away from the scene.

Aggression

Sometimes a male polar bear will try to steal food from another male of equal size. This can lead to conflict. The bears will circle each other with their heads down low and their ears laid back. They will stare directly at each other. This is a sign of aggression. Both bears will chomp with their mouths and make threatening sounds. Often, one of the bears will run off, but sometimes a vicious fight will occur.

Domination

A bear will stand on its hind legs to show its size and to frighten a competitor. Size most often determines which bear is in charge, but this is not always the case. In general, the larger males try to dominate the smaller females, and the females are quick to avoid fighting. Yet an angry mother can scare off even a larger male bear.

Play Fighting

A male will approach another male with his head bowed and his mouth closed. He does not look at the other bear directly. Then, the bears with touch each other around the face. This is called mouthing. When contact has been established, the bears will stand up and try to push each other over, in fun.

Take a Stand

Debate • Research

Photos of polar bears often show the animals in groups, even though group behavior is limited. Is it wrong to portray polar bears as social animals?

Popular movies of polar bears focus on bear families during seasons when cameras can reach them, but the cameras do not follow the bears that are off on their own.

FOR

1. Animals should be portrayed as they really are, not as people want to think of them. Polar bears do not hunt together. If they were truly social, they would form hunting parties.
2. As adults, polar bears keep to themselves unless they are mating or raising cubs. This means they are essentially solitary.

AGAINST

1. Polar bears will share prey, even with bears that are not related. This is a social decision.
2. Young males bond and travel together. Family groups stay together until the cubs are grown.

The **Bear Basics**

Polar bear cubs stay with their mothers for two or three years. Sometimes, a cub will stay with its mother for longer than the normal time period, but this behavior is rare.

When polar bear cubs are about 30 months old, the mother will chase them away. Sometimes, a male bear shows up and does the chasing.

Mating and Birth

Female polar bears do not mate until they are 4 years of age or older. Afterward, they will mate only when they do not have first-year or second-year cubs at their side. Mating between females and males occurs on the sea ice in April or May.

Through a process called **delayed implantation**, the cubs do not start to grow inside the female right away. In preparation for their development, the female will eat a great deal and build up a supply of fat. She may gain more than 440 pounds (200 kg) during the summer. In October, the mother enters a den, where she will experience a state of inactivity called hibernation. During the winter months, her body will use the added fat for food energy. Though her body shuts down in some ways, the fat keeps her alive and the cubs inside her will develop.

A maternity den is where a pregnant female polar bear gives birth and spends several months raising her newborn cubs. The female polar bear usually makes her den in a snowdrift of hard-packed, fine-grained snow. If the female must make her den on land and there is not enough snow, she will dig into the earth. Later, winter weather will cover the den with snow. She digs a long, narrow entrance and then scoops out an inner area about 8 feet (2.4 m) long by 6 feet (1.8 m) wide and 4 feet (1.2 m) high. The snow helps protect against the cold. The temperature inside the den may be 40° Fahrenheit (22° Celsius) warmer than the outside air. In some cases the temperature in the den may even rise just above freezing. Soon, fresh-fallen snow will cover any trace of the den from other animals until the female polar bear is ready to come out with her new cubs.

A polar bear usually gives birth to two cubs. Sometimes, she will have only one cub. Rarely, triplets are born, but it is very hard for the mother to raise all of them. Polar bear cubs are born in December while their mother is in the den and still drowsy from hibernation. The newborn cubs weigh about 21 to 25 ounces (600 to 700 grams). This is roughly the size of a small house cat. The cubs' eyes are not yet open, and their pink skin is covered with a white, fuzzy fur. Despite their helplessness, they are able to use their little claws to climb to their mother's chest for their first feeding. The cubs will then curl up in their mother's fur to keep warm.

Baby Polar Bears

From the moment polar bear cubs are born, their survival depends on their mother. Soon after birth, the cubs will feed on her rich, thick milk. It contains 30 to 40 percent fat, 10 times more than human milk. With such a rich diet, the cubs grow very quickly.

Sometime between late February and the middle of April, the polar bear mother breaks out of her den. For the first few days, the cubs stay inside the den. As they get used to the change, they venture outside. The cubs begin playing with each other and learning about their world of snow and ice. After about two weeks around the den, the mother polar bear leads her cubs out onto the sea ice to hunt for seals. The mother bear helps her cubs get used to the ice. Sometimes, the mother carries her cubs on her back.

Polar bear cubs have a great deal to learn from their mother. She must teach them what to eat, different ways to hunt seals, and how to cope with the many dangers out on the ice. When polar bear cubs leave the maternity den, they are little white bundles of energy, but they are much larger than they were on the day of their birth. The cubs already weigh about 30 times more than when they were born.

Their mother is the only teacher and protector that polar bear cubs will ever know. Her skills and knowledge of the Arctic will be taught to them until they are ready to live on their own. The bears will be ready to hunt by themselves when they are 2 or 3 years old. Until then, their lives are filled with danger, and most will die. Some researchers believe that 70 percent of polar bear cubs do not live to their third birthday.

Polar bear cubs are hairless and blind when born, but they develop quickly.

The **Bear** **Basics**

Beneath its fur, a polar bear's skin is black. This helps its body absorb the heat from the Sun.

A polar bear cub may grow to be more than 750 times larger than when it was born.

The Bear Basics

Scientists can tell how old a polar bear is by removing a tooth. Polar bear teeth have growth rings inside them. A new ring is added to the tooth each year of the bear's life.

Polar bear mothers receive no help from polar bear fathers. The farther north the bears live, the longer the mother must care for her cubs.

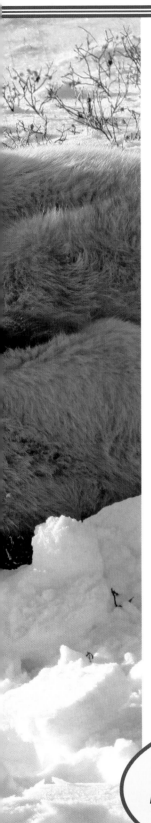

Development

By the end of the first month, the cubs weigh four times more than they did at birth. They can now see and hear. Their first teeth are pushing through. They can crawl but are still unable to walk. During the next couple of months, the cubs become more and more mobile. Even as their mother sleeps in the maternity den, the cubs are beginning to move around. They can walk by the eighth week. The cubs are soon climbing over their mother and each other. Their fur is getting thick, and their little bodies are building a layer of fat to protect them from the cold when they leave the den. When their mother opens the den around the end of the third month, male cubs weigh about 22 to 26 pounds (10 to 12 kg), while female cubs weigh slightly less.

From the fourth to sixth months, the cubs must gain more weight in order to survive in their icy world. When the cubs leave the maternity den, it is windy and cold. The temperature can be −10°F to −40°F (−23°C to −40°C). The cubs stay very close to their mother. She will stop often to nurse the cubs and let them rest. She will not **wean** them until they are more than 2 years old. The young polar bears need the fat and nutrients that the milk provides.

By 6 months of age, male cubs weigh about 90 pounds (41 kg). Female cubs are about 10 pounds (4.5 kg) lighter than males. The cubs are now able to keep up with their mother as she searches for seals. They are also able to swim quite easily. Most polar bear cubs remain with their mother for two years or more, learning the ways of the Arctic. They are then forced to leave and live on their own. Some young bears will stay with their brother or sister or join up with another young bear to live and hunt together for a short period of time.

"No one just walks past a polar bear, even if he or she has seen hundreds before. Every single bear is special and worthy of special appreciation." - Ian Stirling

Ian Stirling, one of the world's leading experts on polar bears, is a senior research scientist with the Canadian Wildlife Service and a professor of zoology at the University of Alberta. He has written a number of books and research articles on polar bears.

Habitat

Polar bears live in the northern parts of Russia, northern Norway, Greenland, northern Canada, and western and northern Alaska. In North America, many polar bears are found at the Beaufort and Chukchi Seas, in Alaska. The farthest south that the bears live year-round is at James Bay, in Canada.

Most scientists call polar bears land mammals. Other scientists consider polar bears to be marine, or sea, mammals. This is because they spend most of their life out on the sea ice and get their food from the sea. Polar bears have been found more than 100 miles (161 km) from any land or ice. More than anything, they like to stay close to their food source, the seals that live in the water. The entire Arctic is the bears' habitat.

Organizing the Arctic

Earth is home to millions of different **organisms**, all of which have specific survival needs. These organisms rely on their environment, or the place where they live, for their survival. All plants and animals have relationships with their environment. They interact with the environment itself, as well as the other plants and animals within the environment. These interactions create **ecosystems**.

Ecosystems can be broken down into levels of organization. These levels range from a single plant or animal to many species of plants and animals living together in an area.

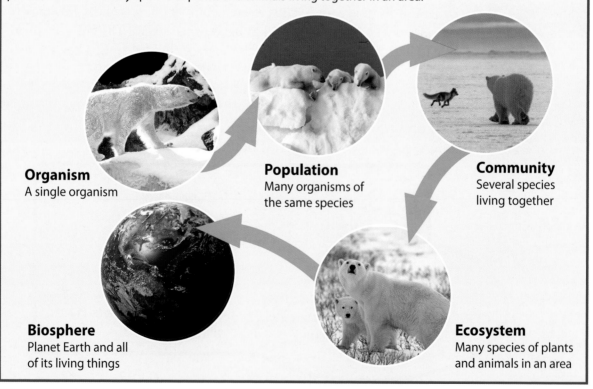

Organism
A single organism

Population
Many organisms of
the same species

Community
Several species
living together

Biosphere
Planet Earth and all
of its living things

Ecosystem
Many species of plants
and animals in an area

The regions in which polar bears live have fewer species of plants and animals than other areas. Each species, therefore, plays a bigger role in keeping the ecosystem healthy.

Range

For most of the year, polar bears live and hunt on the sea ice. A home range is the area an animal travels in during its normal activities of gathering food, mating, and caring for its young. Polar bears have very large home ranges. As they hunt for seals, polar bears travel farther in their lifetime than any other land animal. It has been estimated that the area covered by a polar bear during its lifetime may range from 19,000 to more than 77,000 square miles (50,000 to more than 200,000 square kilometers). Polar bears do not defend their home ranges from other bears. It is normal for the home ranges of individual bears to overlap. As they hunt, polar bears may cover 19 miles (30 km) or more each day searching for seals.

Located at the top of the world, the Arctic includes more than 5 million square miles (12.9 million sq. km) of land and, for most of the year, ice-covered seas. Polar bears are not spread evenly over this vast area. Scientists believe that there are about 19 different **subgroups** of polar bears in the Arctic. These population groupings have developed as a result of ice movement patterns. Each subgroup of polar bears has its own home range but may share part of it with other subgroups. For example, in the Hudson Bay area of Canada, there are three subgroups that share part of the sea ice for hunting. When the ice melts each summer, all the bears in a particular subgroup return to the same area on the shore of Hudson Bay to await the return of cold weather. They will have no contact with bears from other subgroups until the sea freezes again.

While hunting on the sea ice, polar bears travel alone or in a family group consisting of a mother and her cubs.

Polar bears use their sense of smell to tell them if another bear is nearby.

Migration

If possible, polar bears prefer to remain on the ice-covered ocean all through the year. Only while polar bears are out on the sea ice are they able to catch seals. The preferred habitat for polar bears is close to the continental and island coastlines, where the ice melts each summer and is not too thick for hunting seals. Strong winds and ocean currents near the land create open strips of water called leads. These channels or cracks of water may remain free of ice for several minutes or many months. Polynyas, which look like ponds or lakes, dot the sea ice. These pockets of open water never freeze. Seals, whales, walruses, and other marine mammals prefer to live near these bodies of open water.

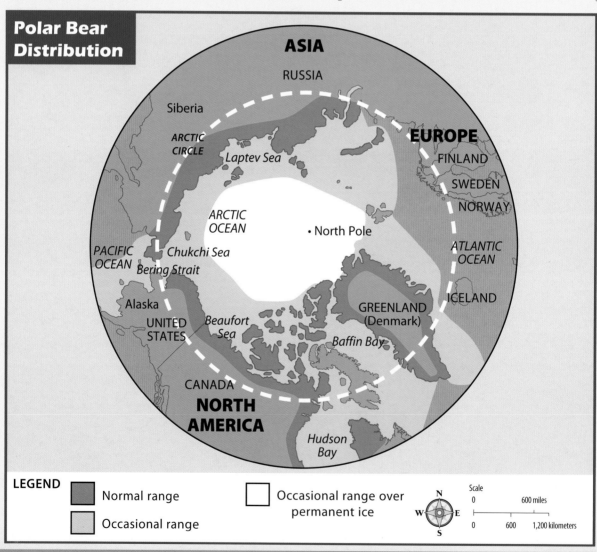

Polar Bear Distribution

ASIA

RUSSIA

Siberia

ARCTIC CIRCLE

Laptev Sea

EUROPE

FINLAND

SWEDEN

NORWAY

ARCTIC OCEAN

• North Pole

ATLANTIC OCEAN

PACIFIC OCEAN

Chukchi Sea

Bering Strait

ICELAND

Alaska

UNITED STATES

Beaufort Sea

GREENLAND (Denmark)

Baffin Bay

CANADA

NORTH AMERICA

Hudson Bay

LEGEND

Normal range

Occasional range

Occasional range over permanent ice

Scale
0   600 miles

N
W   E
S

0   600   1,200 kilometers

When swimming, a polar bear can stay underwater for up to two minutes.

Life for polar bears is a constant search for food. They use sea ice as a platform when hunting, so their hunting grounds are widest in winter. When the weather gets warmer, the ice retreats, and many polar bears move northward with it. For example, the bears at Alaska's Beaufort Sea go north. Other groups of bears, such as those found at Canada's James Bay, are known to stay where they are. The sea ice at James Bay melts by the end of July, and the bears live on shore until late October or November. As soon as cold weather causes the ocean to freeze again, the bears return to the sea ice to continue their search for seals. For bears on shore, food is very hard to find. Many polar bears that spend several months on land will lose more than 500 pounds (227 kg) and look very thin by the end of the summer.

Take a Stand
Debate • Research

Should we stop drilling for gas and oil in the areas where polar bears live?

For thousands of years, only the Inuit and other native peoples lived in the Arctic. Today, companies are drilling for oil and gas under northern land and seas. The human population is growing, as are the region's humanmade problems.

FOR

1. Oil spills and other **pollution** from drilling could kill tiny creatures called algae and anthropods, which live in the sea. Fish that eat these tiny plants and animals, seals that eat the fish, and polar bears that eat the seals would all then have nothing to eat.
2. Humans should learn to use other sources of energy, such as solar energy, instead of oil or gas. They should also learn to use energy more wisely.

AGAINST

1. Humans have to use gas and oil in order to power machines and run their homes and businesses. Other sources of energy are not sufficient to supply all of the energy needed.
2. The Arctic is so big that the land can be shared. Special parks and nature reserves could be set aside for the protection of polar bears, seals, walruses, whales, and other animals.

Diet

Polar bears are **carnivores**. Their preferred meal is the ringed seal. Large adult polar bears can eat up to 90 pounds (41 kg) of food in one meal. They eat the energy-rich fat and skin of the seal first. The meat and other body parts are eaten only if a bear is very hungry. Polar bears will feed on the seal for an hour or more. Younger bears that are just learning to hunt sometimes feed on the catches of older bears.

The ringed seal is so-named because its back is covered with circles of color that look like splattered paint.

Polar bears have many ways of hunting ringed seals. Each fall, as more sea ice forms, the seals prepare holes in the ice, using the claws on their front flippers. These holes are called breathing holes. A seal must keep its breathing hole open all winter in order to have places where it can come up to breathe fresh air every 10 to 15 minutes. Most often, a polar bear will use its sense of smell to find a seal's breathing hole, even if it is covered with snow. The bear will then stand or lie motionless, waiting for the seal to surface. Once the polar bear senses the seal has arrived, it uses its front legs to break through the snow. The bear pins the seal against the side of the breathing hole with its big paws. The polar bear then pulls its prey out of the hole, using its teeth. Polar bears use a similar hunting method to break into the places where seals give birth to their pups in the spring.

In addition to ringed seals, polar bears also hunt the less numerous, but much larger, bearded seals. Bearded seals can weigh 900 pounds (408 kg) or more. Young walruses are also occasionally taken. Adult walruses are usually avoided due to their large size, thick leathery skin, and the danger posed by their large **tusks**. There are also reports of beluga whales or narwhals sometimes being caught by a polar bear.

For polar bears trapped on shore when the sea ice melts each year, there is very little to eat. The bears will mainly try to find **carrion** washed up on shore, birds' eggs, and small rodents such as lemmings and voles. They will also eat berries, edible plants such as kelp and seaweed, and whatever else they can find.

The Bear Basics

The polar bear's long neck allows it to keep its head above water while swimming. It also helps the bear to reach into the holes in the ice where seals are found.

The ringed seal is the smallest seal in the world. It is about 5 feet (1.5 m) long and weighs between 130 and 150 pounds (59 and 68 kg).

The Food Cycle

A food cycle shows how energy in the form of food is passed from one living thing to another. Polar bears are a part of the food cycle from the time they are born through to adulthood. During all the stages of their development, polar bears affect the lives of many other animals. In the diagram below, the arrows show the flow of energy from one living thing to the next through a **food web**.

Decomposers
The body of a dead polar bear often sinks to the bottom of the ocean. Decomposers break down the bear's body, adding nutrients to the ocean that are eaten by even the smallest water creatures.

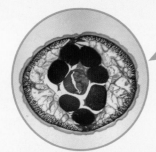

Parasites
Polar bears carry many types of parasites. The bears are often infected by the worm *Trichinella* after eating infected seals.

Tertiary Consumers
The polar bear is usually the top predator in its food web. Few other animals hunt it, although killer whales sometimes eat polar bear cubs as they swim in the water. The polar bear's main sources of food are seals and other secondary consumers.

Producers
Plankton are tiny plants that live in the water. They are eaten by animals that live in the sea.

Primary Consumers
Many types of sea creatures eat plankton in the water, including fish such as cod.

Secondary Consumers
Seals and other marine mammals are the main source of food and energy for polar bears. The seals eat primary consumers.

Take a Stand
·Debate·
·Research·

Does the number of polar bears show that Earth's environmental problems are getting worse?

In some recent years, there has been no change in the overall number of polar bears. In the first decade of the 21st century, however, the total number of polar bears declined.

FOR

1. To show environmental trends, 10 years is a more accurate time period than one or a few years. The fact that polar bear numbers declined over a 10-year period is important.
2. In recent years, the amount of sea ice has decreased due to changes in climate. It makes sense that bear numbers are declining in response, as the sea ice is their hunting ground.

AGAINST

1. Scientists started counting polar bears in the 1960s, and since then the overall number of bears has increased.
2. The number of bears in Alaska has declined, but this can be also linked to illegal hunting.

The **Bear Basics**

On average, a polar bear must catch a ringed seal every five to six days to maintain its body weight.

A polar bear is capable of capturing a large walrus, but this seldom occurs. The animals most often ignore one another when they share the same ice.

Competition

Polar bears are top predators, but they are very careful around large walruses. These marine mammals can measure more than 10 feet (3 m) in length and weigh more than 2,000 pounds (900 kg). In the water, a bull walrus can catch a polar bear with its long ivory tusks. It is also possible for a killer whale to attack a young swimming polar bear. Despite these challenges, neither walruses nor whales can be called competition. The bears know how to live with and avoid these animals. The bears also, to some extent, know how to avoid one another.

The competition among the bears themselves is not as extensive as it could be, given their size and fighting potential. This is because polar bears avoid fighting one another unless they are in danger of starving. As long as there is enough food, polar bears do not feel the need to defend their home ranges from other bears. The fighting that does occur is most often play fighting or competition among males for mates.

Brutal fighting does occur when food is scarce. In these cases, adult male polar bears are a threat to all smaller bears. While on the sea ice, they will sometimes force a smaller bear away from a seal it has caught. If hungry enough, they will even try to eat polar bear cubs. In these cases, the mother bear will try to protect her offspring.

Over time, the main challenges to polar bears have been from humans. The Inuit have lived near polar bears for thousands of years. They have hunted polar bears for food and to make warm clothing from the fur. Before rifles were available, a hunter would use his sled dogs to find and distract a bear while he attempted to spear it. This was very dangerous. For many centuries, Inuit hunting did not affect the overall number of polar bears. In the 20th century, however, polar bear numbers were in serious decline due to severe over-hunting in all the northern nations where the bears lived. Then, in 1973, five nations that have polar bears within their borders came to an agreement. The nations were Norway, Russia, the United States, Canada, and Denmark, which controls Greenland. They agreed on a conservation plan in order to save the bears. It is called the International Agreement on the Conservation of Polar Bears.

Young males play fight in preparation for fighting for mates.

The Bear Basics

Although all bears are classed as carnivores, most bears eat more plants than animals. Polar bears are the most carnivorous of all bears as there are few plants in their environment and they are forced to eat meat.

Polar bears and sled dogs have been seen playing together. The animals sometimes nuzzle each other.

Polar Bears with Other Animals

Polar bears share their snowy home with a number of other animals. One of these is the Arctic fox. These cat-sized animals have brown fur in the summer and snowy white fur in the winter. An Arctic fox will sometimes follow a polar bear for many months while the bear hunts on the sea ice. Sometimes a seal will haul itself out of the water and lie on the ice next to its breathing hole. A bear will sneak up on the seal. Before its prey can slip back into the water, the bear will capture a meal for itself and the fox. Normally, a polar bear eats only the skin and fat of a seal. The Arctic fox **scavenges** the remains.

The way the bears treat their human neighbors relates to how hungry the bears feel. Many of people's early ideas about the vicious nature of polar bears came from stories told by the first explorers in the Arctic. In order to survive, these early explorers ate seal meat, fed seal meat to their sled dogs, and used seal oil to provide heat and light. The smell of dead seals led many hungry polar bears to the explorers' camps. Conflicts between humans and hungry polar bears have resulted in deaths on both sides.

Even today, travelers need to take special precautions in the Arctic. A hungry polar bear will sometimes stalk and attack a human. Often, the bear sneaks up on the person and surprises him or her in the same way that it hunts for seals.

"Polar bears must be respected because of their size, speed, and strength. When in the bear's world, humans must take extreme care to stay out of their way." - Steven Amstrup

Steven Amstrup is a professor and wildlife biologist working with Polar Bears International. Living and working in Alaska, he led a polar bear research team for many years.

Folklore

Many Inuit and other peoples of the Arctic believe that humans have spirits that live on after a person dies. Similarly, they believe that each animal also has a spirit that stays after the animal's death. Polar bears were thought to have one of the most powerful animal spirits. After a successful hunt, the Inuit of King Island in the Bering Sea always held a great feast and performed a "polar bear dance" to show respect and thanks for the bear's giving up its life to the hunter. They were convinced that not showing respect to the polar bear would bring harm to all the people of the tribe.

The early people felt a sense of awe and mystery about the great white bears. Polar bears had the ability to stand on their hind feet, to build dens similar to igloos, and to hunt the same seals that people hunted. The combination of these human-like traits and the bears' ghost-like ability to blend into the snowy environment led to legends of shape-changing. In these stories, the bears took human form. Many legends were instructional guides to inform the listener of the need to respect polar bears or risk great harm.

There are many Inuit stories in which polar bears are treated as if they were people. One of these stories is told in a book called *The Polar Bear Son: An Inuit Tale* by Lydia Dabcovich. The story tells of a lonely old woman without a family. One day she finds an orphaned polar bear that she takes home and adopts as her son. Eventually, her fellow villagers become both jealous and afraid of the bear. The old lady learns they intend to kill him. She helps the polar bear escape. Out of love and kindness toward his adoptive mother, the polar bear continues to visit and look after her.

Inuit legends tell of polar bears teaching people to hunt.

Myth	VS	Fact

Polar bears are lazy and slow.

Polar bears move slowly to save energy. When necessary, they can run very quickly. They have been clocked at more than 30 miles (48 km) per hour. This is faster than an Olympic sprinter. It is also fast enough to catch a caribou. Polar bears reach their top speeds when they are chasing prey or being chased.

Polar bears always attack people and other animals on first sight.

While polar bears can be dangerous, attacks on people are very rare. Polar Bears International reports that in almost all cases when a bear has attacked a person, the bear was stirred up, scared, or hungry.

Polar bears cover their noses with snow to blend in with the landscape, especially when hunting.

While many stories have been told about this tactic, it has not been observed by scientists who study polar bears. Most likely, it is not true or happens very rarely.

The Inuit of Alaska have long told stories about their respect for the fierceness of polar bears. Any hunter who captured a bear with just a spear was honored with a feast.

Status

The polar bear is listed as a threatened species by the U.S. government. This means polar bears are considered at risk of becoming **endangered**. The International Union for Conservation of Nature (IUCN) has placed polar bears on the list of animals it considers at risk. Scientists estimate that there are between 20,000 and 25,000 polar bears living in the Arctic. The IUCN tries to count the number or bears in each of the 19 subpopulations of polar bears. It has found that eight of these populations are declining. Three are stable. One is increasing. Numbers for the other seven subpopulations are unknown.

Research on the changing climate of the Arctic shows that, on average, the weather is getting warmer. As overall temperatures increase, the length of time the sea ice stays frozen each year is declining. Polar bears rely on the thick ice to support them when they search for ringed seals. With the ice freezing later and melting sooner each winter, there is less time for the bears to hunt. Canada has the largest population of polar bears. About 60 percent of polar bears are found in Canada. Researchers for the Canadian Wildlife Service studied polar bears living in the western Hudson Bay region. They reported that female bears weigh less than they used to. The researchers believe that the shorter hunting season on the sea ice is causing the weight loss. These female polar bears are also having fewer cubs because they do not build up enough fat to support themselves and their developing cubs in the maternity den.

When wildlife officials come across cubs whose mothers have died, they often attempt to place the animals in a zoo. In some zoos, the bears are kept in areas that are set up to be similar to the animals' natural habitat. This is not always the case, however. Joint studies by wildlife researchers, zoo staffs, and outside organizations have concluded that there need to be stricter regulations about the areas in zoos where polar bears are kept. The regulations would ensure that polar bear enclosures are big enough for these large bears, have soft walking surfaces that will not hurt the bears' paws, and have private places where the bears can rest out of public view. Large swimming and wading areas filled with clean water must also be available. Zoos would be required to provide air conditioning to ensure the bears do not suffer from overheating. Perhaps one day, all captive polar bears will be housed in facilities similar to the exhibit at the San Diego Zoo in California. This $5 million enclosure even features a stream that is stocked with trout the bears can attempt to catch.

The **Bear** **Basics**

In 2010, the Convention on International Trade in Endangered Species voted to keep polar bears off its list of threatened animals. Declaring the bears threatened would have made it illegal for anyone, including Inuit hunters, to hunt the bears.

The bears in Canada's Hudson Bay region live farther south than other polar bears, which makes it easier for scientists to reach them and study them. These bears are being watched closely for signs of what may happen to the bears farther north.

The Bear Basics

Since the late 1970s, the extent of summer sea ice in the Arctic has become much smaller than before. It has been reduced by an area equal in size to the U.S. states of Alaska, Texas, and Washington combined.

The loss of sea ice is a threat to the world's polar bears. Researchers recently announced that the ice now covers less area than it has at any time in the last 1,450 years.

Saving the Polar Bear

In response to research on polar bears, most countries with land in the Arctic have placed limits on the hunting of polar bears. In Russia, no hunting of polar bears is allowed. An international agreement has also provided for ongoing research on all aspects of the Arctic. Various groups raise money and awareness of the challenges facing the polar bears and ways that people can help.

The town of Churchill claims to be the polar bear capital of the world, and its efforts to help the bears are notable. Located in Manitoba, Canada, Churchill is a small town on the western shore of Hudson Bay. Each July, when warm weather melts the sea ice, 1,000 or more polar bears are trapped on the shores near Churchill for up to four months, until subfreezing temperatures return in the fall. Tourists travel out of the town in special vehicles called tundra buggies so they can watch the polar bears along the shore of Hudson Bay.

Years ago, bears would scavenge at the local garbage dump or walk through the streets of the town looking for food. This led to confrontations between bears and humans that resulted in the deaths of both. Beginning in 1969, the town of Churchill and the provincial wildlife authorities began a program to make the area safe for both bears and humans. This program is called the Polar Bear Alert. The town officials have a series of steps they take to deal with bears that wander in the wrong areas. Some bears are kept in a safe area until they can be released on the ice again. If a female and cubs are involved, they are flown by helicopter to an area in the north, where they will be safe.

From an Expert

"Bears keep me humble. They help me to keep the world in perspective and to understand where I fit on the spectrum of life. We need to preserve the wilderness and its monarchs for ourselves, and for the dreams of children. We should fight for these things as if our life depended upon it, because it does." - Wayne Lynch

Wayne Lynch is a leading wildlife photographer and author. He has long been interested in bears and is the author of *Bears: Monarchs of the Northern Wilderness* and *Bears, Bears, Bears.*

Back from the Brink

Educating people about polar bears and the challenges they face allows us to understand the ways we can make a difference. For thousands of years, the only people living in the Arctic were the Inuit and other native peoples. Today, this has all changed. With extensive gas and oil drilling, other industrial development, and an increase in tourism, new communities have brought many people into direct contact with polar bears for the first time. Officials stress that anyone who goes to an area where polar bears live needs to respect the natural ways of the bears in order to avoid conflict.

- All polar bears, including cubs, can be dangerous and unpredictable. Never try to approach, feed, or disturb a polar bear.
- Try not to travel on foot when it is dark or when visibility is poor. If on foot, travel in a group and make noise so as not to surprise a bear.
- Avoid areas where there is a strong smell or odor, such as at a garbage dump.
- Stay close to the safety of a vehicle or building but away from objects the bears might hide behind.
- Inform wildlife officials immediately if a polar bear is spotted in a restricted area.

Most people will never set foot in the Arctic, but there are many other ways to help polar bears. These include understanding and supporting conservation efforts in the Arctic. Several groups are trying to preserve the sea ice, which is the bears' natural habitat. For more information on efforts to save the polar bear, contact:

World Wildlife Fund
1250 24th Street, NW 20037-1193
P.O. Box 97180
Washington, DC 20090-7180

In 2012, the largest area covered by Arctic sea ice was 237,000 square miles (614,000 sq. km) smaller than the average sea ice area from 1979 to 2000.

Activity

Debating helps people think about ideas thoughtfully and carefully. When people debate, two sides take a different viewpoint on a subject. Each side takes turns presenting arguments to support its view.

Use the Take a Stand sections found throughout this book as a starting point for debate topics. Organize your friends or classmates into two teams. One team will argue in favor of the topic, and the other will argue against. Each team should research the issue thoroughly using reliable sources of information, including books, scientific journals, and trustworthy websites. Take notes of important facts that support your side of the debate. Prepare your argument using these facts to support your opinion.

During the debate, the members of each team are given a set amount of time to make their arguments. The team arguing the For side goes first. They have five minutes to present their case. All members of the team should participate equally. Then, the team arguing the Against side presents its arguments. Each team should take notes of the main points the other team argues.

After both teams have made their arguments, they get three minutes to prepare their **rebuttals**. Teams review their notes from the previous round. The teams focus on trying to disprove each of the main points made by the other team using solid facts. Each team gets three minutes to make its rebuttal. The team arguing the Against side goes first. Students and teachers watching the debate serve as judges. They should try to judge the debate fairly using a standard score sheet, such as the example below.

Criteria	Rate: 1-10	Sample Comments
1. Were the arguments well organized?	8	logical arguments, easy to follow
2. Did team members participate equally?	9	divided time evenly between members
3. Did team members speak loudly and clearly?	3	some members were difficult to hear
4. Were rebuttals specific to the other team's arguments?	6	rebuttals were specific, more facts needed
5. Was respect shown for the other team?	10	all members showed respect to the other team

Quiz

1. What is the scientific name of the polar bear's family?

2. Under a polar bear's white fur, what color is its skin?

3. When polar bears stare directly at each other, what does it mean?

4. What is the usual number of cubs at each birth?

5. When do the cubs' first teeth usually show up?

6. Which season is the best time for the bears to hunt seals?

7. Which people have lived with polar bears for centuries?

8. What feature do polar bears look for on the ice when hunting seals?

9. Which country has more polar bears than any other nation?

10. What climate-related change threatens the polar bear's habitat?

Answers:
1. *Ursidae* 2. black 3. sign of aggression 4. two 5. by the end of the first month
6. winter 7. the Inuit 8. breathing holes 9. Canada 10. loss of sea ice

Key Words

Arctic: the region of Earth around the North Pole where the climate is very cold

blubber: layers of fat in large mammals that live in the sea

camouflage: when an animal's appearance blends in with its environment so that it is very difficult to see

canine: a pointed tooth

carnivores: animals that eat mostly meat

carrion: remains of a dead animal

delayed implantation: a process by which an unborn animal does not begin to grow right away in its mother's womb

dominant: stronger and more powerful than another animal

ecosystems: communities of living things and resources

endangered: a type of plant or animal that exists in such small numbers that it is in danger of no longer surviving in the world

family: one of eight major ranks used to classify animals, between order and genus

food web: connecting food chains that show how energy flows from one organism to another through diet

fossils: bones or other remains or evidence of animals that lived very long ago

mammals: warm-blooded animals that have fur or hair and feed their young milk

order: one of eight major ranks used to classify animals, between class and family

organisms: forms of life

pollution: something that spoils the environment, causing living things to become sick or die

predators: animals that live by killing other animals for food

rebuttals: attempts to counter, or disprove, an argument

retract: to draw back into the body

rudders: flat pieces on the back of boats used for steering

scavenges: finds and eats dead or leftover remains

sea ice: large areas of ice that cover Arctic waters, especially in the winter months

species: groups of individuals with common characteristics

subgroups: secondary groups within a larger group

tusks: enlarged front teeth of certain animals, such as elephants or walruses

wean: when a mother stops giving her milk to her young

Index

Log on to www.av2books.com

AV² by Weigl brings you media enhanced books that support active learning. Go to www.av2books.com, and enter the special code found on page 2 of this book. You will gain access to enriched and enhanced content that supplements and complements this book. Content includes video, audio, weblinks, quizzes, a slide show, and activities.

Audio
Listen to sections of the book read aloud.

Video
Watch informative video clips.

Embedded Weblinks
Gain additional information for research.

Try This!
Complete activities and hands-on experiments.

WHAT'S ONLINE?

Try This!	Embedded Weblinks	Video	EXTRA FEATURES
Chart the levels of organization within the biosphere.	Learn more about polar bears.	Watch a video about polar bears.	**Audio** Listen to sections of the book read aloud.
Map polar bear habitats around the world.	Read about polar bear conservation efforts.	See a polar bear in its natural habitat.	**Key Words** Study vocabulary, and complete a matching word activity.
Complete a food web for polar bears.	Find out more about polar bear habitats.		
Label and describe the parts of the polar bear.	Discover more fascinating facts about polar bears.		**Slide Show** View images and captions, and prepare a presentation.
Classify polar bears using a classification diagram.	Learn more about what you can do to help save polar bears.		**Quizzes** Test your knowledge.

AV² was built to bridge the gap between print and digital. We encourage you to tell us what you like and what you want to see in the future.

Sign up to be an AV² Ambassador at www.av2books.com/ambassador.